A World of Difference

Masks!

By Alice K. Flanagan

CHILDREN'S PRESS®
A Division of Grolier Publishing
New York   London   Hong Kong   Sydney
Danbury, Connecticut

Dedication *For masked dancers of dreams*

Picture Acknowledgements

Cover (globe), NASA; cover (top left), © Lee Boltin/Lee Boltin Picture Library; cover (top right), © Lee Boltin/Boltin Picture Library; cover (right), © Robert Frerck/Odyssey/Chicago; cover (bottom), © Hilarie Kavanagh/Tony Stone Images; 1, © John Elk III; 3 (top), © Reinhard Brucker; 3 (middle), © Boltin Picture Library; 3 (bottom), © Anna E. Zuckerman/ PhotoEdit; 4 (top), Christie's, London/SuperStock ; 4 (bottom), © Kevin Horan/Tony Stone Images; 5 (top), © Robert Frerck/Odyssey/Chicago; 5 (middle) © Walter Frerck/ Odyssey/Chicago; 5 (bottom), © Benjamin DeMarco/SuperStock; 6 (top), © Reinhard Brucker; 6 (bottom), Reinhard Brucker; 7 (top), © Suzanne Murphy/Tony Stone Images; 7 (left), © Boltin Picture Library; 7 (right), © Wolfgang Kaehler; 8 (left), © Tony Morrison/South American Pictures; 8 (right), Gary Conner/PhotoEdit; 9 (top), Cameramann, International; 9 (middle), © Boltin Picture Library; 9 (bottom), © Lee Boltin/Boltin Picture Library; 10 (left), © Lee Boltin/Boltin Picture Library; 10 (right), © John Elk III; 11 (left), © Robert Brenner/ PhotoEdit; 11 (right), © Reinhard Brucker; 12 (left), © The British Museum; 12 (top right), © Wolfgang Kaehler; 12 (bottom right), © Reinhard Brucker; 13 (right), © Kurt Scholz/ SuperStock; 14 (top left), © Corry Larsen, Tony Stone Images; 14 (middle right), © Reinhard Brucker; 15 (top right), © Robert Frerck/ Odyssey/Chicago; 15 (bottom left), © Anna E. Zuckerman/PhotoEdit; 15 (bottom right), © B. Kapoor/ SuperStock; 16 (bottom left), UPI/Bettmann; 16 (middle right), The Bettmann Archive; 17 (top left), Reuters/Bettmann; 17 (bottom right) © David Hiser, Tony Stone Images; 18 (bottom left), © John Elk III; 18 (top right), © Chip & Rosa Maria Peterson; 18 (bottom right), © Tom McCarthy/PhotoEdit; 19 (top right), © Heinz Mollenhauer/Photri; 19 (bottom), Photri; 20 (top right), © Boltin Picture Library; 20 (bottom left), The Bettmann Archive; 21 (top left), North Wind Picture Archives; 21 (bottom right), © Dave G. Houser; 22 (top left), © Roger Lee/SuperStock; 22 (bottom left), © Alain Le Garsmeur/Tony Stone Images; 22 (bottom right), © John Elk III; 23 (top left), American Museum of Natural History, New York/Bridgeman Art Library, London/ SuperStock; 23 (bottom right), Photri; 24 (top right), © Lee Boltin/Boltin Picture Library; 24 (bottom left), Egyptian National Museum, Cairo/SuperStock; 25 (top right), © Reinhard Brucker; 25 (bottom), © Boltin Picture Library; 26 (top right), Austrian Cultural Institute; 26 (bottom right), © Wolfgang Kaehler; 27 (top left), © Wolfgang Kaehler; 27 (bottom right), © Reinhard Brucker; 28 (top right), Photri; 28 (middle), © Robert Frerck/ Odyssey/Chicago; 28 (bottom left), Civic Library of Padua/Mauro Magliani/SuperStock; 29 (top left), © Jonathan Nourok/ PhotoEdit; 29 (top right), © Michael Rosenfeld/Tony Stone Images; 29 (bottom right), SuperStock; 30 (top right), © Victor Englebert; 30 (bottom left), © Robert Frerck/Odyssey/ Chicago; 31 (top right), © Cameramann International, Ltd.; 31 (bottom left), © Collection of F.G. Irvine.

On the cover
Top left: Lega tribe mask, Zaire
Top right: Hopi kachina mask, United States
Bottom left: Theatrical mask, Bali
Bottom right: Chimu burial mask, Peru

On the title page
Theatrical mask, Sri Lanka

Project Editor Shari Joffe
Design Steve Marton
Photo Research Feldman & Associates

Flanagan, Alice.
     Masks! / written by Alice Flanagan.
        p. cm. — (A world of difference)
     Includes index.
     Summary: Examines the various functions of masks around the world.
     ISBN 0-516-08213-2
     1. Masks — Social aspects. — Juvenile literature. [1. Masks.]
  I. Title. II. Series.
  GT 1747.F53 1996
  391`.434 — dc20

                                           95-39672
                                        CIP
                                        AC

Contents

Face-to-Face

Every face tells a story. Look into a mirror, or study another person's face, and watch the unique story unfold. Young or old, happy or sad, mean or kind—faces make you smile, laugh, or cry. They might even make you hide. Cover your face with a mask, and it will change the story. It will affect how you feel and act. It will also influence how others feel and act toward you.

Have you ever worn a mask on Halloween or at Mardi Gras time? Did you have fun disguising who you are and pretending to be someone else? Well, you are not alone. Mask-making and masquerading have played important roles in people's lives all over the world from earliest times to today.

Wooden mask, Gabon
Traditionally, masks have been made from whatever materials are available. This ceremonial mask from the African country of Gabon is made from wood, a popular mask material around the world because of its durability.

Corpus Christi festival, Spain
Masks are a part of many festivals and celebrations around the world. In Toledo, Spain, the Roman Catholic festival of Corpus Christi includes a colorful "Parade of the Giants."

Harvest ceremony, San Ildefonso Pueblo, New Mexico In many cultures, masks are used for religious or ceremonial purposes.

Masks serve many purposes. A mask can entertain audiences, keep alive sacred traditions, or honor ancestral spirits and heroes. It can disguise the wearer and conceal his or her true identity from others. It can also protect the wearer from harm and help him or her to work or play more safely.

In some societies, certain masks are thought to have supernatural powers. The Bangwa of the African country of Cameroon and the Zuni of New Mexico in the southwestern United States are among many groups who believe that when a sacred mask is worn, the wearer is transformed into a spirit. He or she is also given its power.

Around the world, masks play a part in religion, growing up, celebrating, and remembering ancestors. They help people face life or express themselves in a way that they might not be able to, face-to-face.

Arctic surveyor Some masks are worn as protection from freezing temperatures or other dangerous conditions.

Mask Makings

Masks arouse wonder, awe, and fear in us. They are worn in almost every country of the world, from the cold, ice-covered regions of Alaska to the hot tropical jungles of Brazil. The purpose of making masks, as well as the style and materials used, may vary from culture to culture. In fact, masks look as different as the people who wear them. Some masks resemble birds, animals, or human beings. Others look like magical spirits or frightful beings. Some are made of wood, animal hide, plant fiber, corn husks, or fur. Others are made of clay, shells, ivory, metals, or stone.

Seneca corn-husk mask
The Seneca originally lived in the northeastern United States. Corn has special meaning for them, as it was traditionally one of their most important crops. During Midwinter Feast ceremonies, Seneca members of the Husk Face Society don corn-husk masks and dance to ensure a good corn harvest. The masks are made almost entirely of corn husks that are braided and sewn together.

Dance mask, Mali This mask from the African country of Mali is made from cowry shells strung together with plant fiber.

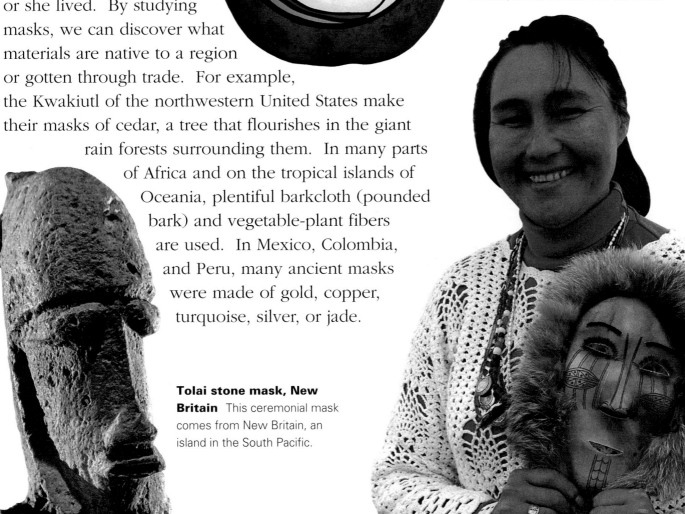

From every mask, we can learn about the mask maker as well as the area of the world where he or she lived. By studying masks, we can discover what materials are native to a region or gotten through trade. For example, the Kwakiutl of the northwestern United States make their masks of cedar, a tree that flourishes in the giant rain forests surrounding them. In many parts of Africa and on the tropical islands of Oceania, plentiful barkcloth (pounded bark) and vegetable-plant fibers are used. In Mexico, Colombia, and Peru, many ancient masks were made of gold, copper, turquoise, silver, or jade.

Gourd mask, Puerto Rico
This painted mask is made from a calabash, a type of gourd native to the tropical island of Puerto Rico.

Yupik dance mask, Alaska
The Yupik, who traditionally have lived in parts of Siberia and Alaska, make masks from the hide and fur of the caribou, an animal native to the arctic.

Tolai stone mask, New Britain This ceremonial mask comes from New Britain, an island in the South Pacific.

Ancient gold mask, Colombia
Before burying their honored dead, the
Ancient Inca of South America covered
the faces of the deceased with gold
masks.

By studying masks, we can also make conclusions about the skill of the artist and how advanced the society is. The ancient iron, bronze, copper, silver, and gold masks of Rome, Egypt, China, Mexico, and South America may tell us that these people were active traders. On the other hand, they might also tell us that they knew how to mine as well as use metals. You see, masks can tell us a lot. So far, what have they told you?

Festival mask, Mexico
Masks can be made from
whatever materials are available
—even something as simple
as a paper plate!

Mud masks, Papua New Guinea Ceremonial masks made from local materials are an important part of many of the cultures of Papua New Guinea, a country in the South Pacific. These masks are molded from mud and clay and are decorated with local berries.

Roman bronze mask, c.100 A.D.

Aztec turquoise mosaic mask, Mexico, c. 1200-1500 To honor their dead rulers, ancient Aztecs made elaborate face masks of them, which they decorated with precious stones.

Calling the Spirits

When you were small, you probably asked your parents questions about everything you saw. Where does the sun go at night? Who makes it rain? From earliest times, people have wondered about the world around them. Their search for answers about the forces that control life led them to believe in spirits. Long ago, people believed that good and evil spirits lived in the animals, the water, the earth, and the sky. They tried to please the spirits. Some even thought about how to capture them so that they could possess their power. With such power, they could cure the sick, control the weather, and defeat their enemies.

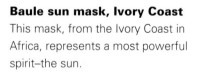

Baule sun mask, Ivory Coast
This mask, from the Ivory Coast in Africa, represents a most powerful spirit–the sun.

Songye mask, Zaire Some masks are worn to invoke harmful spirits that will frighten people enough to keep them from doing wrong. Among the Songye people, a masquerader traditionally kept law and order in villages by threatening to inflict evil on those who broke rules.

Tlingit animal spirit masks The Tlingit of the Northwest Coast of North America belong to clans named the Raven, the Eagle, and the Wolf. During winter feasts called *potlatches,* the Tlingit invoke these powerful animal spirits while they dance wearing masks made in their images.

Shaman performing a religious ritual, Fiji In many cultures, masks represent—or are even thought to actually contain—powerful spirits. Often, only a few chosen people in the community, called shamans, are allowed to possess the power.

And so, early people gave names to the spirits and imitated the animals and the magical beings whose powers they wished to possess. They made spirit masks and hoped that wearing them would make the spirits happy. Perhaps, they thought, the masks would even bring the spirits to them. In time, dances and ceremonies accompanied mask wearing. Eventually, only a few chosen men and women earned the right to perform the sacred ceremonies and possess the power of the masks.

Ancient rock paintings found in North America and Africa of masked hunters give us clues about who the first mask wearers were. These hunters believed that they could lure the spirits of the animals by wearing face masks and mimicking animal movements. Later, they wore animal skins and heads to conceal themselves and get close to their prey.

Eventually, using masks to cure sickness and keep away evil became important. It is still one of the primary purposes of masks. In Sri Lanka, an island southeast of India, Thovil priests are called upon to cure the sick. Wearing the demon masks, they conduct elaborate ceremonies to break the spells of *yakas* (demons) and heal or bring peace of mind to the sick. In Canada and the northeastern United States, Seneca Indians who are members of the False Face Society carve masks from living trees to capture the tree's spirit and its power to cure. When cut away

Baining spirit masks, Papua New Guinea These barkcloth masks, used in nighttime ceremonies, represent various animals and plants.

Sanni mask, Sri Lanka In Sri Lanka, Thovil priests conduct a night-long curing ceremony in which dancers may wear one of 18 different *sanni* masks representing demon spirits responsible for causing specific diseases. Each ceremony usually concentrates on the most important disease demon to be driven out. This mask is worn to cure deafness.

Seneca False Face masks False Face masks are treated with great respect in Seneca society. After being used, they are wrapped in white cloth and carefully stored face down.

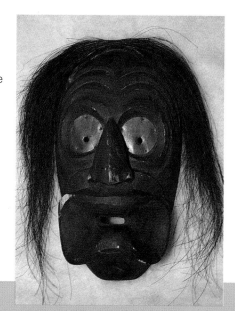

Rangda mask, Bali, Indonesia This mask represents Rangda, the widow of the king of Bali, who became a witch in the eleventh century. Rangda's bulging eyes, fanged teeth, monkey-like ears, and protruding tongue make her a frightening sight.

from the tree, the masks are painted and worn in ceremonies to cure the sick and help hunters and travelers.

When misfortune threatens villagers on the island of Bali, Indonesia, some perform the Rangda dance. In this ceremony, one masked dancer becomes Rangda, the queen of witches. Others join in and plead with her to spare them from misfortune.

Yoruba *Gelede* mask, Nigeria Any Yoruban man can participate in the secret *Gelede* society, which helps maintain the health and prosperity of the community through masked ceremonies handed down from the ancestors. In these ceremonies, men dress as full-figured women and wear wooden masks that represent Iya Nea, the Great Mother of all life.

Initiation ceremony, Liberia Masqueraders in the secret Poro Society of Liberia, Africa, resemble huge beasts. They pretend to capture boys and swallow them up. This symbolizes their loss of boyhood and their emergence as adults.

In many cultures, including several communities of West Africa, masks play an important role in preparing boys and girls to be adults. The ceremonies, which are performed by the secret *Poro* society for men and the secret *Sande* society for women, are called initiation rites. Masked beings lead boys and girls through certain practices that teach them the traditions and skills that will make them adults in their society.

Among many agricultural communities, masked ceremonies help ensure that crops grow well and harvests are good. In pueblo villages of the dry Arizona desert of the southwestern United States, the Hopi people dance

Vendaval fertility mask, Brazil This mask is used in a ceremony to ensure that the crops will grow well.

for the *kachinas* (spirits) to bring rain for gardens of corn, beans, and squash. Each dancer wears a mask that represents a different *kachina* and carries with him prayers for peace, a successful harvest, and good health. On another continent, the Yoruba people of Nigeria, in Africa, conduct magnificent masquerade ceremonies to please the Great Mother Iya Nea. Yorubans believe that Iya Nea can influence the size and health of their families and harvests.

In many parts of the world, beliefs and customs have changed. But our questions haven't. We are still asking the same questions about life that our ancestors did. Masks remain a very important link to them.

Hopi *kachina* mask The Hopi believe in spirits called *kachinas* that take the form of animals and other natural phenomena. The *kachinas*, who first brought rain to the Pueblos, are said to have left their masks behind when sent to dwell in the bottom of a desert lake. When dancers put on the *kachina* masks, they actually become the *kachina* spirits who have returned to help bring rain. This mask represents the buffalo *kachina*.

Veiled women, India Brides in China, India, and Morocco wear veils that cover their faces during wedding ceremonies. The practice developed from an earlier custom of disguising the bride to protect her from spirits threatening to endanger the wedding. In some countries, women always remain veiled in public.

The Merry Masquerade

Everyone loves a parade! Don't you? And everyone loves to celebrate! So just grab your costume and put on your mask. Come join the fun of a masquerade ball, a circus show, or a Mardi Gras parade! Don't forget New Year's Eve, carnival time, and Halloween. And take some time to wonder about how these celebrations came to be.

Most masked celebrations we enjoy today were once important religious ceremonies. Some were performed to welcome the first day of spring or the beginning of a new year. Others honored the memory of a god or a saint, or an important historical event such as Independence Day. In some areas of the world, these celebrations still continue.

In the little mountain village of Imst, Austria, a spring festival takes place every three years. Giant masked characters reenact

Sculpture of the Roman god Janus

New Year's Eve ball, United States The tradition of wearing masks on New Year's Eve may have come from the ancient Roman custom of honoring the god Janus, the god of gates and doors and of beginnings and endings. Janus had two faces. He looked both ahead and backward at the same time.

***Tigre* mask, Mexico** The *tigre,* which is one of the most popular masks made in modern Mexico, is worn in the famous *tigre* dance during fiesta entertainment.

Tibetan *cham* masks and dancers In Tibet, before the start of a new year, Buddhist monks perform the masked *cham* dance to drive out demons and evil spirits. In the dance of *Chojeh,* the Lord of the Dead, monks wear a mask that looks like a bull with bulging eyes and sharp teeth. Between its horns is a row of five yellow skulls.

the struggle between spring and winter for control of nature. In Mexico, the *tigre* (jaguar) dance is an important part of fiesta entertainment. During it, masked performers impersonate the jaguar, the guardian spirit of ancient Aztec warriors. Buddhist monks in Tibetan settlements of India and Nepal observe each new year with the masked *cham* dance that drives away demons and evil spirits. Everyone joins in by offering greetings of "good luck" for the coming year.

Halloween, which is a popular holiday in the United States, originated from a Celtic festival for the dead. In time, some of the practices of the Celtic festival became part of the Christian holiday of All Hallows' Eve, the night before All Saints' Day.

Another popular festival is Carnival, held every year in the cities of many European, Latin American, and Caribbean countries. In Nice, France, and other places with a French influence, such as New Orleans, Louisiana, this period of merrymaking is called Mardi Gras. The custom comes from the Roman Catholic practice of feasting before beginning a forty-day period of fasting (Lent) in preparation for Easter. Wearing masks during Carnival gives participants the freedom to act in ways that ordinarily would not be proper.

Dance of the Conquest, Guatemala A masked parade is part of a yearly folk festival observed in Latin American countries to commemorate the arrival of the Spanish conquistadors in America in the 1500s.

Halloween masks, United States

Mask worn for Ladakhi festival, India

Carnival masks, Venice, Italy

***Fasching,* Germany** In Germany, Carnival is called *Fasching.*
The origin of masks worn at Carnival time is uncertain, although
it may have imitated local festival practices, which often included
mask-wearing.

Mystery, Comedy, and Storytelling

Remember when you played a game called "Peek-a-boo" with a baby brother or sister? They watched in wonder while you hid your face behind a mask made by your hands. A moment later, your face popped out and you cried "peek-a-boo!" In delight or fright, your brother or sister laughed or cried. Well, people have been repeating this activity for thousands of years. Eventually, it made its way to the stage, as actors began using masks to create characters other than themselves.

Japanese *Nō* wood mask Lacquered wood masks of Japanese *Nō* musical dramas are made with great detail. There are several hundred different masks in *Nō* plays. They are worn only by male performers.

In ancient civilizations, heroic figures, beautiful women, and frightening animals were the first kinds of masks to be worn by performers. On the continent of Europe, the earliest theater masks can be traced to Greece in the sixth century B.C. There, in huge outdoor arenas, masked Greek actors reenacted the popular legends of gods and goddesses. The plays, which were called comedies or tragedies, were usually accompanied by masked musicians and a large masked chorus of singers.

Sculpture of Ancient Greek comedy mask Because early Greek masks were made from perishable materials, such as canvas and cork, they have not survived. However, we know how they look from ancient sculptures and paintings.

Drawing of a Medieval mystery play In England, organizations called trade guilds built stages on wagons that they moved throughout the town.

In northern Europe, Catholic priests of the early Christian church wore masks to dramatize Bible stories and stories of the saints. In 1207, when Pope Innocent III forbade the clergy from wearing masks in church, lay people performed the plays in the churchyard. They were called miracle plays and mystery plays. A masked character that occurred often in these plays was the devil. He could look like a cat, a scary monster, or an ugly, old man.

Today, European masked theater has all but died out. However, in parts of Asia and among Native North Americans living along the Northwest coast of the United States and Canada, masked dancers still perform storytelling traditions that have evolved from sacred ceremonies. In China, Buddhist and Taoist priests continue the ancient custom of donning masks and performing plays that encourage people to follow Buddhist teachings. In Japan, the famous wooden *Nō* masks are still worn in the musical dramas that depict rice-planting and harvesting rituals. They have remained unchanged since the sixteenth century.

Gombey Dancers, Bermuda Bermuda is a self-governing British colony. Most of its people are descendants of slaves brought from Africa by the British in the 1600s and 1700s. Some of the folklore of Africa has been preserved by the Gombey Dancers, who, on public holidays, wear elaborate masked costumes and perform African-inspired dances to the strong rhythms of drums.

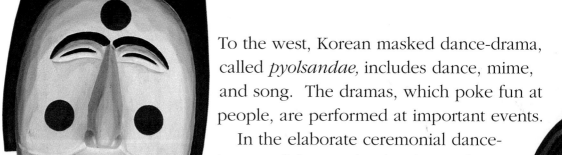

Korean *pyolsandae* mask

The Korean *pyolsandae* began as entertainment for foreign visitors in the palaces of Korean rulers. When the rulers stopped paying the performers, the performers brought the theater to farms and villages.

To the west, Korean masked dance-drama, called *pyolsandae,* includes dance, mime, and song. The dramas, which poke fun at people, are performed at important events.

In the elaborate ceremonial dance-dramas of the Kwakiutl Indians of Canada and Northwestern United States, masked theater is at its best. Their dramatic wooden masks with movable parts are often two or three masks in one. As the outer mask folds back, it reveals the mask of a human face within. This kind of mask may have developed from the belief that at one time some human beings had power to change into animals and back again.

Buddhist religious play, Bhutan

Kwakiutl transformation mask Some of the masks carved by Northwest Coast Indians are hinged and open to reveal another mask inside—transforming the performer into another spirit. Often, only the owner of the mask knows why and how it was made.

Snake-demon *kolam* mask, Sri Lanka There are two forms of masks in Sri Lanka: *sanni,* used in curing rituals; and *kolam,* used in secular (non-religious) dance-dramas. *Kolam* is said to have originated when the Hindu god of good fortune carved entertaining *kolam* masks to cheer up a sad Indian queen. The snake-demon is one of the most popular characters in *kolam* performances.

Dance-drama mask, India In India, masks are most often used in dance-dramas that are a part of springtime folk festivals.

Honoring Our Ancestors

Did you ever think about why we put pictures or statues of people important to us in places of honor? One reason is to keep alive their memory. Belief in an afterlife was and still is widespread among peoples of the world. At one time, masks played a central role in many burial ceremonies. Evidence of this fact has been found on every continent but Antarctica.

The Aleuts of Alaska placed a mask over the faces of their dead to protect them from the dangerous glances of spirits as they journeyed to the next life. Ancient Egyptians and the Chimu of Peru buried favorite possessions with their dead so that they would feel at home in the new life. They also placed painted plaster and wooden masks over the faces of their dead, believing that a mask preserved the personality and helped the soul

Chimu burial mask, Peru, A.D. 800-1470 The Chimu of Peru covered the faces of their dead rulers with gold masks. Sometimes these masks were decorated with red paint and feathers.

Burial mask of King Tutankhamen of Egypt, 1342 B.C. This gold mask of Tutankhamen of Egypt is a good likeness of the young king. The heads of a cobra (symbol of Lower Egypt) and a vulture (symbol of Upper Egypt) on Tutankhamen's forehead show that he was ruler of all Egypt.

on its travels to the other world. It also identified the person so that the wandering soul could always find its body.

The Aztecs of central Mexico and the Maya people of southern Mexico placed pottery dogs in their tombs. The dog-gods, which looked like today's Chihuahuas wearing human masks, made faithful companions and guides for the souls of the dead.

In France, during the fifteenth century, wax masks were made of deceased kings to preserve a lasting image of them. After a king died, an artist made a mask of his face, complete with real hair and beard. The mask was attached to a life-size dummy of the king dressed in royal clothing. It was then put on display so that people could pay their respects.

Masked Mayan pottery dog, Mexico
This small pottery dog is from an ancient tomb in Mexico. The dog is wearing a mask, which indicates that he was a god.

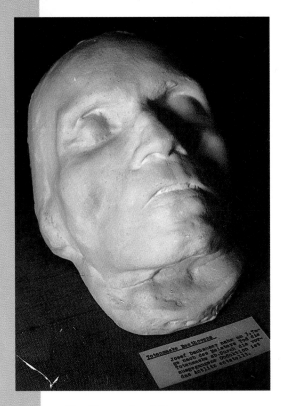

Death mask of German composer Ludwig van Beethoven, 1827
From the 1600s to the 1900s, making death masks of famous people was popular in many parts of Europe.

Over the centuries, masks have been made of many prominent people after they died. Sometimes, these people made masks of themselves while they were living. George Washington, the first president of the United States, had a plaster life mask made of himself.

Today, in many parts of the world, especially in Africa and on islands in the South Pacific, some people believe that the spirits of their dead ancestors live among them. They conduct elaborate ceremonies to convince the spirits to help them in life. Others try to persuade them to go away.

On the island of New Ireland, in the South Pacific, ceremonies are held each year to honor the returning masked spirits of the dead and ask for their help.

Irian Jaya masks, Indonesia
Among the people of Irian Jaya, huge plant-fiber masks like this are used in ceremonies honoring a person who has recently died. Impersonating the spirit of the dead ancestor, the mask-wearer appears for the last time before his kinsmen. After the ceremony, the mask-wearer will often adopt the children of the deceased.

Dogon masks, Mali Masked dances of the Dogon people are held at funerals and at special ceremonies that take place every two or three years. Called *Dama* ceremonies, these rituals lead the spirits of the dead to the ancestors. There are more than seventy different types of Dogon masks used in the ceremonies. Best known is the tall *kanaga* mask, which represents a bird.

Tatanua **mask, New Ireland** This type of mask from New Ireland, an island in the South Pacific, is used to contact the spirits of dead ancestors. Each *tatanua* mask represents a deceased person and is given his name.

In contrast, during the funeral rites of some African tribes, the spirit of the deceased is sent on his way and asked not to return. After a New Guinea funeral, masks and other dance equipment are sometimes placed on a raft and floated downriver. It is hoped that the raft will sink, and the spirit of the dead person will be transformed into a sea animal.

In most cultures today, people are placing less and less importance on the value of ancestors in their lives. The future seems more important than the past. Cameras and computers are changing the way we preserve people's memories. Do you think they might even change our need for masks?

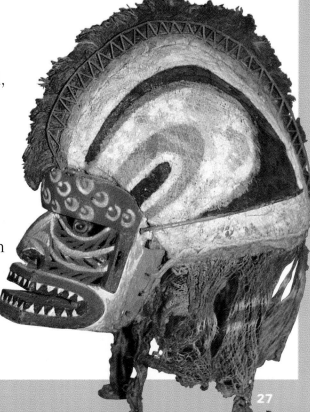

Protective Masks

Did you know that armored masks once protected European knights in battle? During the Middle Ages, soldiers, and even their horses, wore heavy metal armor into battle. The armor, made of bronze and iron, covered the entire body from head to toe. The head was protected by a helmet with a face mask called a visor.

During the 1500s, Japanese *samurai* warriors wore terrifying metal masks. The masks were designed not only to protect them but also to frighten their enemies. Masks concealed their emotions and gave them better control over their enemies.

Japanese armored mask, 1500s
The purpose of Japanese war masks was to protect the wearer and frighten the enemy.

Today, masks play an important role in protecting people in daily life. Surgeons and nurses wear masks to protect themselves and the patients they serve from the spread of deadly germs. In the dangerous environment of space, astronauts wear pressurized suits and helmets. Without oxygen, which the mask provides, astronauts would certainly die.

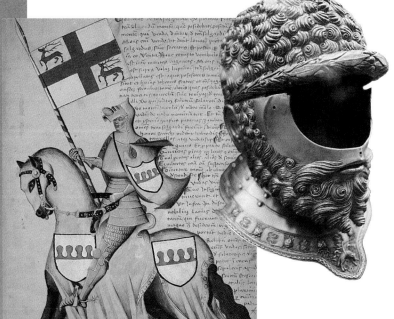

Medieval knight in armor, Italy (left), Spain (above)
European knights wore heavy armor into battle during the Middle Ages. Although it was meant to protect them, it often prevented them from moving well.

Welder, United States Welders wear masks to protect themselves from the harmful light and flying sparks.

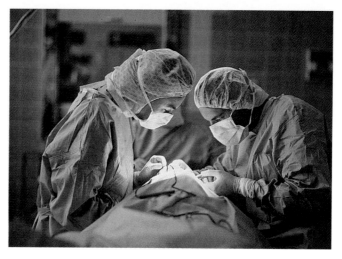

Doctors performing surgery While in the operating room of a hospital, surgeons and nurses wear masks to decrease the chances of spreading germs.

In ocean exploration, divers also wear pressurized suits and helmets. The specialized masks allow them to breathe underwater for long periods of time. Welders wear masks, too. But their masks have a special lens that protects their eyes from the intense light produced by the welding. Even firefighters and soldiers sometimes wear masks to keep them from inhaling hazardous smoke and poisonous gas.

Safety masks are standard equipment in some sports. Baseball catchers, football players, hockey goalkeepers, and snorkelers all wear masks for protection. Can you describe other masks that are worn for war, work, or play?

Hockey goalkeeper, Canada To protect themselves from severe injuries caused by contact with fast-flying pucks, hockey goalkeepers wear masks.

Masked Heroes

Heroes who wear masks to humbly conceal their identity have appeared in the literature and history of many cultures throughout the world. Today, through the magic of television and movie theaters, people everywhere can enjoy the masked performances of popular heroes and fictional characters of modern times. In the United States, there are many famous fictional masked crimefighters: the Lone Ranger, Batman, the Teenage Mutant Ninja Turtles, and Power Rangers, to name a few.

In Mexico, *Superbarrio* confronts evildoers. In Japan, *Anpanman* helps those who are hungry. Every culture has its modern heroes.

Batman Batman is one of many American superheroes fighting for justice. The masked character first appeared in comic books in the 1950s and was brought to the movie screen in the 1980s.

Subcomandante Marcos doll, Mexico The mysterious rebel fighter known only as "Subcomandante Marcos" is a real-life masked hero to the Mayan Indians of Chiapas, Mexico. In 1994, he led a revolt against the region's landowners, who had long been unfair to the Mayans working for them. Marcos always wore a bandanna to conceal his identity.

Anpanman mask, Japan

Often, comic-book characters are turned into masks so that children can pretend to be their favorite superhero. Originally created in 1973 in Japan, *Anpanman* is a hero made out of a popular Japanese food— a bean-paste bun. *Anpanman* helps the hungry by giving them part of his bean-paste body to eat. He also battles the evil *Baikinman,* who tries to spread disease and pollute the environment.

Toy store with various superhero masks, Japan

They represent life today, but they have their roots in the past. They are new versions of characters even primitive people recognized—animals and beings with power to control good and evil, life and death. Masks will always have universal appeal. They will always fill a need to remember our heroes, answer our questions, and keep mystery alive through disguise.

Glossary

accompany to go along with (p. 11)

ancestral having to do with relatives from the past (p. 5)

caribou reindeer (p. 7)

ceremony a series of acts performed in some regular order according to custom (p.4)

civilization a complex society with a stable food supply, division of labor, some form of government, and a highly developed culture (p. 20)

conceal to hide (p. 5)

cowry a type of shell found in warm seas (p. 6)

culture the beliefs and customs of a group of people that are passed from one generation to another (p. 27)

custom the usual way of doing things among a people or culture (p. 21)

deceased dead (p. 25)

durability ability to last (p. 4)

elaborate having much detail (p. 12)

hazardous dangerous (p. 29)

identity the way a person views himself or herself (p. 5)

impersonate imitate (p. 17)

invoke bring forth (p. 10)

lacquered coated with a smooth finish (p. 20)

masquerade a party or event at which people wear masks to disguise themselves. (p. 16)

masquerading wearing a disguise to pretend to be something or someone other than oneself (p. 4)

mimicking imitating (p. 12)

native born, grown, or originating in a particular place or country (p. 7)

perishable liable to spoil or decay (p. 20)

phenomena observable facts or events (p. 15)

prominent important (p. 26)

protruding sticking out (p. 13)

resemble to look like (p. 6)

sacred holy (p. 5)

significance importance (p. 19)

spirit a supernatural or divine being (p. 5)

supernatural outside the known laws or forces of nature (p. 5)

symbolic standing for or representing something (p. 9)

traditional handed down from generation to generation (p.4)

unique one of a kind, unusual (p. 4)

Index

About the Author

Alice Flanagan is a freelance writer, working out of her home in Chicago, Illinois. Once a teacher, she now enjoys writing for children. Her themes appeal to all cultures and reflect the multicultural nature of society.